Alaska's Dog Heroes

True Stories of Remarkable Canines

Shelley Gill

Illustrated by Robin James

little bigfoot

An imprint of Sasquatch Books | Seattle

In memory of Gabe and Trek—my
two personal dog heroes

Manufactured in China by Midas Printing
International Ltd. (Hong Kong), in
September 2019

Little Bigfoot with colophon is a registered
trademark of Penguin Random House LLC

Published by Little Bigfoot
An imprint of Sasquatch Books
21 20 19   9 8 7

Editors: Gary Luke and Christy Cox
Project editor: Nancy W. Cortelyou
Design: Anna Goldstein

Library of Congress Cataloging-
in-Publication Data is available.

ISBN: 978-1-57061-909-0 (paperback)
ISBN: 978-1-57061-947-2 (hardcover)

Sasquatch Books
1904 Third Avenue, Suite 710
Seattle, WA 98101
(206) 467-4300
SasquatchBooks.com

Introduction

ALASKA'S DOG HEROES work hard. They guard against wolves and bears. They haul everything from train cars to wagons and sleds. They can pack a winter's worth of supplies over mountains and find their way through whiteout blizzards. They can catch criminals, locate kids buried in snow, and sense if it's safe to travel across sea ice. They make split-second decisions that save lives. Of all their jobs, sometimes the most important one is to provide comfort and friendship on dark, cold snowy nights.

The stories you will find in the pages of this book celebrate some of Alaska's most famous dogs and the important jobs they've performed. So go ahead and snuggle with your favorite pup as you read about these courageous dog heroes from Alaska.

Balto

BALTO, AN ALASKAN husky mix, born in 1919, became one of the most famous dogs in the world.

In winters, Balto helped draw heavy freight sleds. In summers, he pulled the pupmobile: a wheeled wagon that was used on the rail tracks around Nome. He was just another working dog.

But in the winter of 1925 the city of Nome was threatened by a deadly outbreak of diphtheria. The only medicine that could stop the epidemic was in Anchorage, more than 1,000 miles away.

The serum was wrapped in furs to keep it from freezing and shipped on a train as far as Nenana. After that, mushers and their dogs lined up along the route to transport the serum from Nenana to Nome—674 miles across some of the toughest and coldest terrain on earth.

Each driver handed off the serum to the next—like a relay race. The lives of the people of Nome depended on the speed of these dogs and their mushers.

Balto, musher Gunnar Kaasen, and the rest of their team completed the final 55 mile leg of the relay. They carried the life-saving medicine into Nome at 5:30 a.m. on February 2. When the town awoke, Balto and Kaasen were given a hero's welcome.

Kaasen said he couldn't have done it without Balto; the dog led the team safely through the night despite a blizzard that made it nearly impossible to see.

A bronze statue of Balto still stands in New York City's Central Park. The inscription reads:
ENDURANCE FIDELITY INTELLIGENCE

In Alaska's territory days, anywhere there were railroad tracks there were also pupmobiles, wagons pulled by dog power. They traveled on train tracks laid during the gold rush.

Togo

TOGO WAS A SMALL black, brown, and gray Siberian husky. He was named after a Japanese admiral. Togo belonged to the fastest musher in Alaska, Leonhard Seppala, known as the King of the Trail.

Like Balto, Togo is famous for his role in the 1925 serum run that saved Nome from diptheria. But Togo was Seppala's best leader.

Twenty different dog teams carried the serum across Alaska but none as far as Togo's. Together Togo and the rest of Seppala's dogs raced up the coast of Norton Sound on a dangerous shortcut.

To save time, they risked crossing a stretch of unreliable sea ice that could have broken loose and floated out to sea. They covered 300 miles fighting blown out trail and 60-below-zero temperatures.

Seppala said Togo was "the best dog to ever travel the Alaskan trail." In addition to the life-saving Great Race of Mercy to Nome, Togo led Seppala's team in three consecutive Alaska Sweepstake championships.

Today, Togo's stuffed remains are on display at the Iditarod Trail Headquarters in Wasilla, Alaska.

Tekla

BEFORE SUSAN BUTCHER became famous for winning the Iditarod Trail Sled Dog Race four times in the 1980s and 1990s, she was an unknown dog musher who lived in the Wrangell Mountains. Her dog team was a mixed bunch except for its leader, Tekla.

Tekla seemed to have a sixth sense. It was as though she could hear Butcher's thoughts. If Butcher thought, "We need more wood," Tekla would lead the team to the woodpile.

However, once when Tekla was a new leader, she defied Butcher's command to "go ahead." Butcher couldn't understand Tekla's disobedience until the dog bolted off the trail just as an ice bridge collapsed into open water. Tekla's instincts saved them. From then on Butcher knew Tekla was her best partner—and for good reason. Tekla would save her life again.

In Butcher's first Iditarod in 1978, Tekla led the team to a nineteenth place finish. The next spring, with Joe Redington, they completed the first and only ascent of 20,300 foot Mt. Denali by dog team.

Redington's team was led by Candy, another accomplished husky, but 14,000-feet up they combined the two teams. With Tekla in the lead, Butcher and Redington arrived at the summit. When they reached the top, the team, affected by the high altitude, would have kept going if not for Tekla. The dog dug in and kept the rest of the straining huskies from overrunning her and plunging off the peak.

Tramp and Red

IN THE LATE 1950S, a fifty-square-mile floating chunk of ice northwest of Barrow, Alaska, served as the site of a scientific camp. One January morning the commander of the base, Colonel Feathers, finished his breakfast and walked out of the mess hall just as a giant polar bear emerged from the icy mists.

Feathers did what most of us would do. He ran! The bear chased him. The bear was gaining on the desperate Feathers when Tramp, a young sled dog that worked at the camp, appeared out of nowhere and attacked the bear. Despite Tramp's courage, Feathers still faced grave danger. With its giant paws, the bear threw Tramp aside, breaking several of the dog's ribs and leaving him alive but unconscious on the ground.

Then Tramp's mate, Red, dove into the fight to protect Feathers and Tramp. Fur flew! There was so much commotion, the weather observer, Bert Reynolds, ran out of his tent to see what was happening. He shot at the bear, careful not to hit Red. The shots alerted more armed men just in the nick of time.

Within moments the bear was dead, and the men rushed to give Tramp and Red first aid for their wounds. Both dogs recovered and two weeks later, Red increased the canine camp population when she gave birth to a litter of seven healthy pups.

Julian, Susitna, and Kashwitna

DURING THE GOLD RUSH in the 1890s, a miner could only enter the Yukon Territory if he brought along a year's worth of food and supplies. That's a lot to carry! The miners used dogs to help them take their provisions over the very steep Chilkoot Trail into the Klondike.

In the spring of 1896, a majestic two-hundred-pound yellow mastiff named Julian packed load after load up the trail. Later he set the record for pulling the heaviest weight of any dog in the Klondike.

Today there are weight-pulling events that memorialize the dogs of the gold rush. One event is called the Fur Rendezvous. The heaviest single pulls (one dog and one load) recorded in Alaska happened at these events in the 1970s. Susitna and Kashwitna, two incredibly strong Saint Bernards—and father and son—pulled 5,220 pounds each, over twenty times their own weight.

Stickeen

IN THE SUMMER OF 1880 the naturalist John Muir and a crew of native paddlers set out from Fort Wrangell to explore Glacier Bay. With them, curled up between the boxes and the baggage, rode a short-legged, shaggy, black, foxlike dog—quite unusual for a northern dog. He was named Stickeen, after the Stickeen Indian tribe.

As the travelers explored the wilds of southeastern Alaska, Stickeen was always ready for adventure. The small dog never seemed to mind breaking trail; enduring storms, rain, and snow; or even encountering the giant brown bears along the shores of Glacier Bay.

One evening Muir and Stickeen were trying to get back to camp after exploring a vast glacier when a terrible storm arose. As they rushed in the direction of the camp, they came upon a huge crevasse. There was only a thin bridge of ice, deep below, where the two could cross. Muir carved descending steps into the ice to reach the bridge, then climbed across the dangerous opening. But Stickeen refused to cross. Normally a quiet, dignified animal, he howled his fear into the night.

Muir begged the little dog to come to him. After much encouragement, Stickeen finally leaped down the icy stairs and skittered across the icy bridge. Then he clambered up the other side of the crevasse toward Muir's outstretched hand.

Muir had never seen such happiness in an animal. Stickeen had gone from absolute despair to unbounded joy. Stickeen was "shouting, swirling round and round in giddy loops." Muir thought the little dog might die of excitement.

After that day, Stickeen would not leave Muir's side or accept food from anybody else during the rest of the time they were together in Alaska.

Hotfoot

THE IDITAROD TRAIL Sled Dog Race is credited with saving the sled dog. Without this famous race, the dogs would've been replaced by snowmobiles.

The dream of Joe Redington Sr. of Knik, Alaska, the first Iditarod took place in March 1973. It was run along old mail trails that hadn't been used for fifty years. The route was a staggering 1,150 miles—from Anchorage to Nome. Few people expected dogs to be able to go the distance—climbing mountains, fighting storms, battling the cold on the Yukon River and the wind on the coast.

It took musher Dick Wilmarth from Red Devil, Alaska, just over twenty days to win the race. He gave all the credit to his lead dog, Hotfoot. Wilmarth said all he had to do was "stay on the sled and let Hotfoot pick the way."

Gratitude and love for great lead dogs has echoed throughout the forty-year history of the famous race.

Patsy Ann

PATSY ANN WAS A bull terrier brought to Juneau, Alaska, in 1929 to be a family pet. But she had other ideas. This funny-faced white dog became the official greeter at the docks during the 1930s.

Patsy Ann had no permanent address. She spent most of her nights at the longshoremen's hall, and her meals came from chefs who toiled in kitchens and galleys all over Juneau. Each evening she made her rounds collecting treats. Everyone fed her so much that in her later years she got very plump.

In those days, a ship coming to dock was an event. Folks would gather at the wharf to watch the ship come in. Long before it was in sight or the steam whistle blew, Patsy Ann somehow always sensed when a ship was coming. She even knew where it would tie up and waited patiently there. What makes this so miraculous is that she was stone deaf from birth!

One time a group of people was waiting for a ship at the wrong dock. Patsy Ann stared at them for a moment, then trotted to the correct dock, guiding them there.

Patsy Ann died peacefully in her sleep at the longshoremen's hall on March 30, 1942. The day after, the townspeople watched as her little coffin was lowered into Gastineau Channel.

Today, a statue of Patsy Ann sits on the wharf. She watches and waits for a ship to sail in, just like she did so many years ago.

Jippi and Blues

JIPPI AND BLUES are two sleek border collies. They are dog detectives currently being trained by Shell Oil to sniff out oil spills beneath Arctic Ocean ice. Scientists hope dogs like Jippi and Blues can alert them to trouble before pollution spreads.

Some dogs have a sense of smell a thousand times better than a human. Dogs can sniff out just about anything. They can smell cancer before doctors can detect it. Dogs can help find avalanche victims and lost kids across Alaska. They can catch criminals. And they can even help scientists locate the scat of orca whales and other endangered species for study.

Now, dogs might be on the front lines of protecting the environment by finding oil spills under a blanket of ice.

Brown and Bruce

SOMETIMES ONLY A small footnote in history is left to celebrate heroes.

There's a dog-eared, musty photograph in the collection of the Alaska State Library. It shows a cold, snowy landscape, a sled with a bundled up driver, and two big, floppy-eared huskies staring at the camera. The driver of the sled was P. E. Larss, a photographer. The picture is dated 1898.

The following words are written on the picture:

Brown & Bruce, the famous dog team that has beaten all records of mountain climbing and long distance traveling in the Arctic and Yukon districts.

Brown and Bruce may not be in many of the history books; the specifics of their fame are lost to time. But someone thought they were special enough to honor them with that photograph so Brown and Bruce wouldn't be forgotten.

Anna

PAM FLOWERS WAS the first woman to cross the Arctic alone. She would not have made it without her little dog Anna.

Flowers trained hard for her 2,500-mile expedition mushing from Point Barrow, Alaska, to Repulse Bay, Canada. She picked only the best dogs to go with her. Her trusted leader Douggie headed her eight-dog team.

Anna was one of two swing dogs and though she was small, Flowers liked how hard she worked. Anna made up for her size with attitude and determination. Week after week Flowers and her dogs traveled over ice ridges, skirting crevasses and open water. The trip took its toll on the team. Food started to run short, and then her leader, Douggie, disappeared! When Flowers finally found him, he was exhausted. He couldn't lead the team anymore.

From then on, it was up to Anna. Across deadly shifting ice, through storms, with her head down and her tail tucked, Anna led. It was Anna who, digging deep, finally pulled the team safely into Repulse Bay on January 9, 1994—more than a year after they'd begun their historic journey.

Buddy

IN APRIL 2010 the Alaska State Troopers presented a specially engraved dog bowl and a big rawhide bone to Buddy, a courageous and smart German shepherd.

Buddy and his owner, Ben, were in the family workshop when a spark ignited some nearby gasoline. Ben's clothes caught fire, and his face got burned. After the man and his dog escaped the burning building, Ben yelled to Buddy, "We need to get help!"

Buddy took off, running through the woods. He found a trooper who was responding to a call about the fire, but had gotten lost. Buddy led the officer back to the house through the maze of winding back roads.

Because of Buddy, the trooper was able to guide firefighters to the scene and save Buddy's family's home. Everyone thought Buddy was amazing, especially since he'd never had any training for emergencies. He just knew what to do to help Ben.

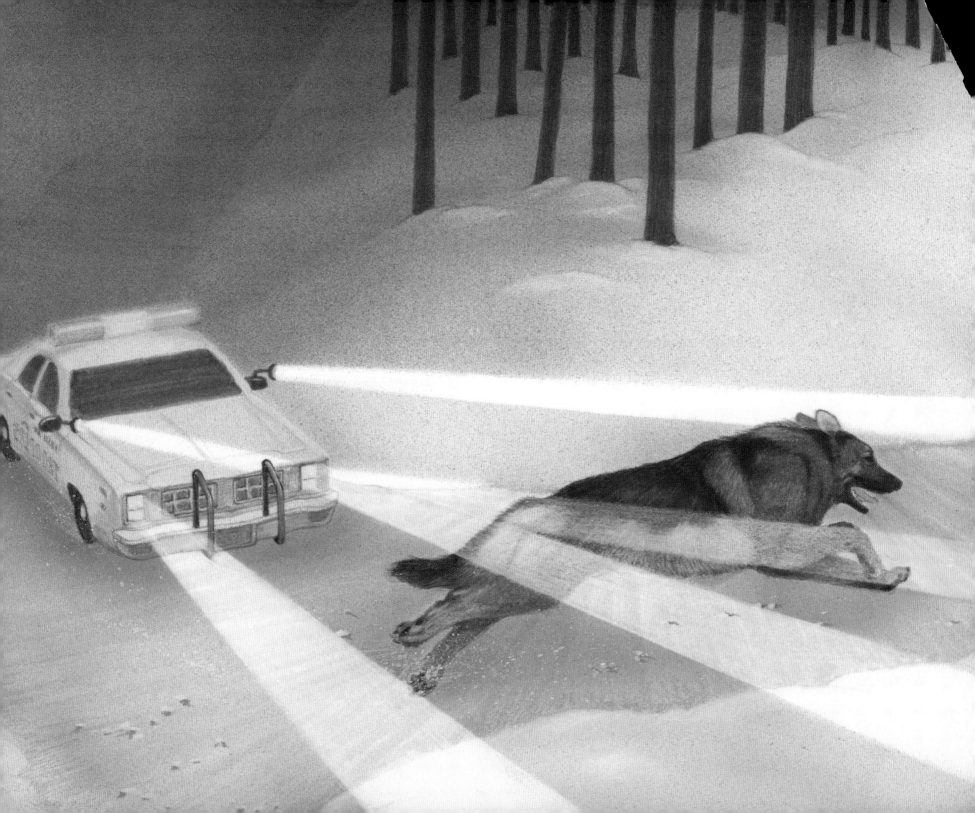

Dugan

IN 1985 LIBBY RIDDLES, an unknown musher from Teller, Alaska, took a trail-hardened dog team into the teeth of a coastal storm to try and win the Iditarod Trail Sled Dog Race.

The year before Riddles's attempt, an experienced Iditarod musher nearly died in a similar storm out on the ice of Norton Sound. Riddles knew she couldn't make any mistakes. So she put Dugan and Axle the Wonder Dog in double lead.

Darkness finally stopped them far out on the ice. Riddles wriggled into her sled tent, crawled into her sleeping bag, and, buffeted by a howling wind, spent a cold, sleepless night.

At dawn, she rousted her team from their warm beds beneath the snow, and they took off for Koyuk. Dugan led directly into the biting wind on a straight course, head down and tug line tight.

The rest is history! The headlines of the Anchorage Daily News screamed, "LIBBY DID IT!" Riddles had become the first woman to win the Iditarod Race as well as the Humanitarian Award for taking the best care of her dogs. Dugan and another leader, Sister, won the Golden Harness Award.

King David

ON A WINTER day in 1986 six-year-old Joey Mays had been missing from his East Anchorage home for hours. His family feared that he might have been kidnapped. Anchorage police officer Gary Gilliam and his K-9 King David were on the case.

The officer and King David began their search right away. The German shepherd sniffed his way down the road. He suddenly stopped and started barking, then began digging frantically in a huge snow berm. When the hole was big enough, Officer Gilliam reached inside. His fingers met two icy feet.

They were Joey's feet. A passing snowplow had buried the boy deep in the snow while he was building a snow cave. Only a tiny air pocket saved him from suffocating.

When Joey was taken to the hospital with hypothermia, he kept asking, "Where is the dog?" So Joey's doctors called Officer Gilliam and asked him to bring King David to the hospital. Joey was overjoyed to meet and hug his hero.

Soon after, King David was awarded the National Dog Hero of the Year Award for his spectacular rescue.

About the Author

SHELLEY GILL was one of the first women to race in and complete the Iditarod Sled Dog Race. She is the author of many bestselling children's books on Alaska and the Pacific Northwest. She lives in Homer, Alaska, writing books and working as a humpback whale researcher in Prince William Sound.

About the Illustrator

ROBIN JAMES has illustrated more than 80 books, including all of the titles in the much-loved Serendipity series. She loves illustrating animals and is currently on the board of directors of Greyhound Pets, Inc. A native of the Pacific Northwest, she lives with her husband in Snohomish, Washington, along with a flock of pet chickens, a herd of horses, and a pack of greyhounds.